POEMS OF HOPE FOR OUR TURBULENT TIME

Amarachi Ruth

Amarachi Film Production & Publishing

Published by
Amarachi Film Production & Publishing
P. O. Box 190973
Roxbury, MA. 02119-0020
Phone: (617)288-5868
Fax: (617)4364691
(800)417-1540

Printed and bound by
Acme Bookbinding Charlestown, MA

I S B N 0-9701116-1-4

Printed in the United States
First Printing

Acknowledgements

I thank God for my parents Ezema Uduma Ikpa and Roseline. I loved them dearly. I have deep and fond memories of them. They were rare individuals. They were very kind, sacrificial, and intelligent. They loved their fellow human beings and were moved to human suffering. They taught us so much and loved us so much; myself, my brothers and sisters. I have tried to alert parents in my book "The Nanny Crisis in America: The Abandoned Children," the crucial nature of loving their children and creating time for them. That was bequeathed to me, and that is why I am who I am today by the Grace of God.

I also thank my kind uncle Chief O. U. Ikpa, former Nigerian Ambassador to Sudan, who loved and cared for my family after my father's untimely death. Without him, we could not have survived. He cared for us like his own children. I also extend my warmest thanks to my sponsor Lawyer Patrick Abuka. Not only did he sponsor me, but was very kind to me during my studies at Prairie Bible Institute, Three Hills, Alberta, Canada.

I dedicate this second book to my blind mother. She was my friend during my turbulent teen life. She counseled me kindly and was always there for me. I loved her with all my heart. My father called her "Enyia," meaning my friend. Enyia, I will see you someday.

INTRODUCTION

We live in a turbulent time in world history. It calls for a time of reflection: reflection on the value systems we have succumbed to that is shaping the way we think: ungodliness, ruthless political ambition, love for power, money, sex, and the negligence of the poor; instead of following the way of the truth.

The result is that many people in our societies are very sad and fearful of the future; homes are crumbling, children are ignored and neglected, many single women bear the burden of raising children by themselves.

When our homes are in turmoil, then our schools, churches, corporations, offices, governments will not be safe and secure. Children, women and the elderly people need to be taken care of. We must find them and help them. We must resort back to the old ways of helping one another, helping nations and other countries of the world, who live in great poverty and destitution.

This book brings hope to people in this peculiar time that we live in. They are reminded not to be afraid, but to put their trust in the Lord, and not men.

TO MY BELOVED MOTHER

You are wise
       Kind
       Rich
       Beautiful
       Tall
       Elegant
Your body, like a stature
Was meant for the gods
Suddenly, your light snuffed out
Your surrounding darkened
You did not age
You struggled to conquer
You battled and lost

You said though my light snuffs out
 I can feel my surroundings
 I can hear voices
Like the deer seeks water
You sat and waited at the
       Door
For humanity to pass by
To share your kindness

You gave all
 You gave yourself
You refused to clip
Your wings
You spread them on
To fly
Souring like an eagle
To freedom

For truly you found
Freedom
Though, your light snuffed out
For in your freedom
You conquered darkness
You enlightened darkness
Your radiance adorned our hearts
And embellished it perpetually

You are my love
You taught me
To love
To forgive
To be kind
To be true
Life can only bear
One of your kind
You are a gift from
          God
You torched many hearts
You are my mother

Contents

Poems Of Hope For Our Turbulent Time

Child abuse

When I hear of a child abused
Then I know a child crushed inside

                and
I see a child masquerade outside
        Then I wonder who she is

Sexual abuse

It is easy to be
    angry
    bitter
    resentful
    unforgiving
    recounting hurts
    holding grudges

    but
You must forgive
to be released
to be healed
to be whole

    remember
there is no other way
to be healed
to be whole
to be released

Aging

Human dilemma
Dreadful intrusion
Despised by society
Abhorred by women
Feared by men
Mocked by youth
Do you have favor at all
Conqueror of human body
Frailty your battle
Loneliness your compassion
Do you have favor at all
Yes, silver hair full of wisdom
Experienced graced in riches
Perception adorned in discernment
Do you have favor at all
My favor lies in acceptance

Glory of the beach

It's quiet
It's peaceful
I lay still
To absorb the peace
The stillness of time
The large body of waters
Whose end meets the horizon
As if infinity

      oh
The calmness
The paradox
Under the calmness
Are creatures of all kinds
Creatures of all species
Living below
Melting with the quietness

The ducks swimming quietly
The sea gulls flying undisturbed
The birds hopping around for food
The fish popping its head now and then

      then
The sunset
Like the rainbow
Spreading like the heavens
Lightening the surface of the waters
Sparkling like a twinkling star
Over the waters

I wonder
What heaven will be like
When I behold His glory
The calmness of the waters
The beauty of the sunset
The lushness of the beach
The mystery below the waters
Teeming with all kinds of sea animals
Like a cover up

      so
 We behold the glory
Of the Lord faintly on the beach
Heavens will be greater beauty
Heavens will be greater joy
When I behold His glory
For the beach is a little of His glory

Beauty in the inside

Beauty is beautiful
She is often admired by men
I often wonder why beauty
Falls by the wayside
I often wonder
What is beauty
When my face is blooming
When my eyes are seductive
When my lips are suckling
When my body is curved

      but
I wonder
Why do men reject me
When my face is blooming
But my heart does not bloom
I am ugly inside
My beauty hides my inside

      Oh
I want to be beautiful inside
I want to be quiet inside
I want to speak kind words outside
I want to do kind deeds outside
That makes me beautiful inside
That makes me enduring inside

Black mind

Black mind
      Is powerful
      Intelligent
      Creative
     Resourceful
      Free

      and
Can build empires
Has built empires
Can rise above the skies
Can do anything she chooses

      but
She is not united
Unity is power
Nations, families, individuals
Not united
Will never rise to power
Will never rise to their dreams

Bonding with a child

Who cares when I
    Need care
When I need care
    Who cares
Who guarantees her
    Presence
When I need care
My bonding secures
    Who is there
When I need care

Children & abandonment

My little angels they say
Are the joys of my life
I live for my little angels

but
When its time to give
Your best to little angels
Your time
Your presence

then
None is found
Little angels wonder away
Lost in confusion
Until lost without remedy

oh
Your time so precious
Is what your little angels need
To grow wisely
Not your money
Not your gifts

but
Your precious time
Your precious presence

Choices

The choices we make
Everyday
Small or big
Determine   our destiny
 Someday
In pursuits of life's ambitions
We hurry and make choices
Choices wrong and detrimental
Choices selfish and exploitive
Choices destructive and lustful
 In the end
Choices wrong
Strangle , maim and destroy

           but
Take time to make choices
Choices right and uplifting
Choices noble and worthy
Choices kind and considerate
Choices sacrificial and progressive

            oh
remember
Choices we make today
Small or big
Determine our destiny someday

Avoiding my conscience

Avoid my conscience
When darkness dims
When confusion looms
When sin knocks
My light obscures
 My plight puddles
My path obstructs
Until restoration occurs
My light obscures

Consideration for my neighbor

When I consider my neighbor
I think of myself
I refrain from myself
To hurt myself

When I consider my neighbor
I think oh, I love myself
I want to be careful
To hurt myself

When I consider my neighbor
I think of myself
I know I want the best for myself
That is how
I consider my neighbor
I want the best for her

Death is not the end

Is it the end
I wonder
    rationalists, critics
    pragmatists, skeptics
    humanists, philosophers
    politicians, economists
    doctors, lawyers, new agers
    psychics, psychologists
    you have nothing to say
    what do you say
    is it the end
     I wonder

        oh
tell me
is it the end
the still lifeless body
the well decorated body
the finiteness of solitude
the wondering
I wonder

Is it the end
I wonder

sleep like death
death a permanent sleep
soul escapes to rest
soul escapes to condemn
body like a fine powder
escapes to sand

is it the end
I wonder
It is not the end
I wonder

Dying

Don't be afraid to die
Prepare with care
Don't forget death snaps
Sometimes in the midst of life
So prepare with care

      not
Your will
Living sensuous
Worldly accumulation
Greedy
Like a vulture

      but
Confession of Lord as Savior
 Loving Him
Loving your neighbor
Keeping God's commands

      then
 You will not be afraid
When you face death

Divorce

When enlightened man
abandoned the divine
        presence
marriage crumbled
at the alter of
        greed

Education

Some think
We are higher animals
Some are lower animals

      but
I often wonder
Why higher are lower animals
Then the mind wonders
Away from higher
And are lower animals

      so
I wonder
Where can I find
The higher animals
Made in the image of God
Not in the image of man

      oh
 Higher animals are
Homes of nurture
In the mind of nurture
Out side the home of torture
Then the mind wonders
Into higher pasture
Derived by the Divine

then
They are higher animals
I wonder
What is higher animals

What is education

What is education
I wonder
Much learning
Much reading
Accumulation of facts
Intellectual pursuits
Scholarly pursuits
Knowledge of the world
Knowledge of the senses

     but
What is education
As I behold the educated man
He did not make sound judgment
He did not make wise judgment
He didn't understand
He let the home burn
He let the school burn
He let the nation burn
He let the world burn

     then
I wonder
What is education
The one in the highest education
The one in the highest scholarship

The one in the highest seat
The one with the highest intellect
He did not understand
He let the home burn
He let the school burn
He let the nation burn
He let the world burn

oh
I wonder what is education
Education is understanding
Understanding of wisdom
Wisdom that starts at home
When we are born
When I learn values at home
And uphold it as I grow
Education is knowledge
When I learn about God
And His laws and uphold it
As I grow
Education is wisdom
When I understand others
And treat them like myself

remember
Education is not only accumulated facts
Education is not only of the intellectual facts
Education is not only of the scholarly facts

        but
Also the knowledge of God
It makes me understand
It makes me wise
It grows my mind and body
It makes me whole

When fear grips the mind

I trembled violently
My spirit fled like a dear
My body drenched like rain
Like one doped
The apparition arrested
My lips
My eyes
My hands
My legs
And put the fire out
She plods on
Grins like a wild cat
Grins like a hawk
She plods on
My spirit fled
I yielded to God

Feminism

From the beginning
You are free
You are equal
You are endowed

    until
Some faulty sage
Some hasty sage
Chains your age

    but
You are free my chains
Like a bird you sing
Who soars high

    for
For your wings spread
Further than the eagles
Away from home

    who
Defiles my fountain
Like a sour grape

My home burns
Like a sour rape

     then
I hear a whimper
A tiny whipper
Weeping
I hear a whimper
A huge whipper
Looming

     oh
 I wonder
Are you free my chains
From the beginning
You are free
You are equal
You are endowed

     Yet
My heart clouds
For some heaviness inside
For want of wisdom inside

Food

Don't eat too much
You have too much
When there is food
Don't eat too much

     oh
Don't eat too much
You have too much
You eat yourself
And forget yourself

     that
Makes me sad
And makes me heavy
And makes my mind heavy
And I go to sleep
And my body is heavy
And I remember nothing

     then
When I wake up in the morning
I am a stump
That slumps

Forgiving others

A little of this virtue
brightens the home, schools, offices
and every corner of the world

A little of this virtue
purges my mind
heals my body

     and
sets me free

to
     love
     create
     grow
     and be my best

     but
None of this virtue
Creeps

fear
anger
resentment
  guilt

that spurs me

to
        hate
        Kill
        destroy

  and
my life stumps

Freedom

Freedom

    Loved by everyone
   Sought by everyone
    Least understood by everyone
    Empires, kingdoms, nations, kings
    Princes, rich and poor
  Perished for want of freedom
   Won by guns and bombs
   Won by speeches and eloquence
   Won by riches and fame
    Won by democracy
   Who won freedom
   Truth won freedom

Gangs

They long for acceptance
Who does not
They long for fulfillment
Of promises made
Who does not

      oh
Despised
Rejected
Frustrated
Feared

They fight
They kill
They rob

      and
The mind dwindles
Lofty ideals banished
Intellect rut in ashes
Like a wondering spirit
In dreams

      so
They hunt for help
Sporadic dress and action

A mark peculiar
For recognition

    for
Society not to
Forget them
Still hoping

    that
 Someone will not give up
Until equality
Becomes actuality

Goals

When I wonder off
The set path
When I am bored and pressured
When I am bitter and angry
When I feel no purpose in life
You set me back on track
To aim
To aspire
To endure
To trust
You make life
Fun and challenging

God is in control

When I wake up in the morning
I wonder where I have been
I have been to another world
Out of reach of human control
It reminds me that someone controls

      my mind
      my body
      my life

I realize I am nothing
I own nothing
God owns everything
He is in control

Guns

The silent watcher waits
In silence she lies
The killer toy
Waiting for the intruder
Can I really protect you
The killer toy wonders
I am possessed by many
Who kill not the enemy
Who is the enemy
The owner asks
The enemy the imagination
Disarm me
Destroy me
The killer toy begs
For I have destroyed
Nations, families and friends
How asks the owner
Wipe imagination
Imprint peace in the imagination
And you will disarm me
And you will destroy me

Hard times

Hard times are always
The best times in our lives
We don't always see
The hidden glory of our trials
Changing us to be more like Jesus

     peaceful
     forgiving
     loving

     and
Growing in wisdom
So we may glorify Him

Home is where it starts

Home is where it starts
When we are born
The shaping of the mind
The neglect of the mind
Home is where it starts

The peace you enjoy someday
The confusion that engulfs someday
The storms that you crush someday
The defeat that drowns
Home is where it starts

The love that spurs you through life to love
The bitterness that stirs you through life to hate
Home is where it starts

destiny
failure
success
strength
courage
hope
Home is where it starts

so
Home is real
Home must not be neglected
empires
nations
schools
corporations
churches
Rise and fall
When there is no home
Crumble when there is no home

oh
Its foolishness
When home crumbles
Its fool hardiness
When home crumbles
Nothing is the same
The heart crumbles
When home crumbles
Destinies change
Home is the cradle of civilization
Home is where it starts
When we are born

Homelessness

I am sitting and wondering why
Why I wonder
Of destinies
Of fate
Of whys
I wonder why
Then the shivering cold
Tumbles the cold wind
Like a frozen corpse
I lay still
Wondering why

      but
Why Lord
I don't understand
I am helpless
I am hopeless
      It's cold
      It's hot

It is the same
I wonder in infinity

     then
They rush by
Rushing humans

Like the rushing wind
They throw their pennies
And rush by

oh
They mutter
Toil and idle not
They mutter
Oh, it could be you
If Grace rush not by

Hope

You are soft like a bed
I nestle on your cushions
When the waves crush
Like an earthquake
When my eyes are dim with longing
When I can hardly understand myself
When I don't know what to do
I rest on your vast and secure arms
Sometimes, you are illusive
Sometimes, you are untouchable
And I wonder where you are
Yet, you are stability
I forfeit my stature without you
I crumble without you
With you there is another day
With you I wait another day
Until there is no another day

Human relationship

Human relationships
Whether they be
marriages
friendships
relations
co workers
parents

oh
they grow
they refresh
they endure

when
we learn
to forgive
to forget
wrongs and hurts

Hunger that satisfies

I know a hunger
A hunger that denies satisfaction
Satisfaction of joy

I know a hunger
A hunger that denies satisfaction
Dissatisfaction that breeds pain

I will seek the hunger
The hunger that satisfies
The hunger that sanctifies

     oh
It is the hunger
The hunger for righteousness
When I do the right thing
It is the hunger
The hunger for righteousness

     then
I will be satisfied
Here and above
I will be satisfied
When I see His glory

Kindness to others

Kindness is the highest state of man
When his mind is exalted
When his mind is joyful

because
He made someone happy
He changed circumstances
He changed destinies
He acted like God
He did the will of God

oh
Kindness is the essence of life
The centre of gravity
The joy of life
The freshness of youth
They are joyful who are kind
They are blessed who are kind
They are rewarded who are kind

Life & reflections

I have often wondered
What is life
You wake up in the morning
You
    eat
    rush to work
    merry
    sleep

    so
What again
I wonder
Is that the end of life
It doesn't make sense

    but
What is life
Some say it is nothing
Some say it is a dream
Some say it is meaningless
 We
    eat
    work
    merry
    die

oh
What is life
It makes sense
When you look inside you
See beauty and peace
Seek beauty and peace

because
The spirit inside you
Made like God
Rises above matter
To love
The greatest gift
Possessed by man
To change himself
To change his world
To rise above matter

Life & reflections

What is life
A tunnel dark, long and weary
A winding path with surprises
Sometimes, a joyful face
Sometimes, a sad face
Each of us
With a blend of each
Joy or sad

      but
    With a mind
    Surrendered
     Trusting
     Resigned

The Divine transforms
The blend
Joy or sad
The way He sees best
For His glory

Life & reflections

When it is all said and done
At the end of the day
You will relax
You will reflect on your deeds
Your reflections will disturb
Your reflections will hurt

    or
They will heal
They will nurture

    oh
Don't be like the cobweb
Shrouded in comfort
Didn't remember
Deeds done
At the end of the day
Evil or good
Will be rewarded
Good or evil

Love & reflections

What is love
I love you
The common way
The common thing
The thoughtless thing

   but
When object of my love
Fails my desire
My love dies
My love fades

   then
I wonder
What is love
When my love
Is not love
I wonder

   oh
Love is deep
Like the ocean
Deep with pain
Pain of acceptance

Bruises of forgiveness
Endurance of time
A deepening of love
A true friendship
With the one I love
Oh, I wonder
What is love

Love & reflections

Love

Must be

    true

Love

Must be

    forgiving

Love

Must be

    unbroken

Love must not be otherwise

Marriage

Marriage a gift from God, the Divine
To sinful mortals
To foretaste the joys of heaven
The greatest bond of friendship
Crowned with genuine affection
Laced with tender understanding
Cemented with true love
Must never be consummated lightly
Demands humble approach
To remain in harmony

The creator saw man's desperation
For friendship and companion
He created the woman
To comfort and help
Not to compete ad frustrate
But to humble submission
To remain in harmony

Man, says the Divine
Protect and love
Love her like yourself
Man, the Divine asks

Understand what this means
Whoever hates himself
Must be insane himself

Did man understand
Counsel of the Divine
To protect and love her
Love sees no wrong
The Divine asks again
Understand what it means
Why discard her
If you love her like yourself
Whoever hates himself
Must be insane himself

Woman, humble yourself
To your man
The Divine warns
Here lies your earthly bliss
Here lies your eternal bliss
Stamp of God's approval
Unsophisticated, powerless, uneducated
Without fame
Though the man
She to humble submission
To remain in harmony
Insightful feminine orders
Powerful the women's liberation

Are mirages of freedom
Though divine guideline
Obsolete may seem
Divine wisdom wins battle
Marriage demands
Humble submission
To remain in harmony

How peaceful, how healing
Our torn homes will be
Should sinful mortals
Seek once again
Divine guideline for marriage
Creator knows best
Needs of sinful mortals
Marriage demands
Humble submission
To remain in harmony

Memory of a loved one

If I can only forget
I keep remembering
I keep remembering her
Like a volcano she erupts
My heart vibrates
Does the grave chain
The spirit
Dear God tell me
Does the spirit live
When grave empty lies
If I can only forget
The day she died
I will see her again
I will forget

My mind

I love my mind
God gave it to me
    To think right
    To speak kindly
    To act considerately

I love my mind
God gave it to me
    To love
    To forget
    To forgive

I love my mind
God gave it to me
    To keep clean
    To create
    To produce
    To distribute
    For His glory

Moral law

I want to throw you off
You choke me to death
You strangle me
You set boundaries that
I cannot reach
I jump over your fitters
I break your head in pieces
Oh, I am bruised, I am bruised
I am chained
I am death
I am wriggling like a snake
I am dying
I will not throw you off
For you set me free

Move on

Move on
No matter what
Tragedy upsets our lives
Plans are shattered
Loved ones die
Children disappoint us
Parents are taken away
Close friends desert us
Divorce destroy marriages
Future plans lost in dreams
Good jobs suddenly taken away

     move on
Tragedy squeezes
The best in us
Like we squeeze out
The juice we love
Tragedy strengthens our faith
And leads to wisdom
The way designed by God
So we are more like Him

Pain

The best moments of our lives are mingled with

pain

A fact if accepted diminishes the pain we bear
For pain is inextricable to human consciousness
And will be over at finality of death

but

There is someone who sustains us in times of
pain

That person is our heavenly father
The Lord Jesus Christ

When pain mocks

Suddenly
You twist
Like daggers thrust inside
Like you are dying inside
You groan
You scream
You plead
For someone to help
For someone to pull the daggers out
No one listens
Nothing happens
Why you mutter
No one answers

     dagger
Stabbed and plunged inside
Plowing like mutiny
Trickling like scanty rain on hot summer
As if someone sets fire inside

     oh
You cannot stop them
Ageless intruder

Invisible creatures of torture
That cannot define nurture
Surrendering cripples torture
Invisible creature of torture

Peace & my mind

When my mind
Is free
Free of guilt
Free of resentment
Free of bitterness
Free of jealousy
Free of turbulence
Free and quiet
Free and relaxed
Purged and sanctified

      then
Then the Lord comes in
To create peace
For He alone creates peace
For it is not given
To the sons of men
To create peace

      oh
The Lord alone creates peace
When the mind is purged
 When the mind is sanctified

that
Is what I think
When I remember peace

In thy Presence

The best time in my life
Is in thy presence
In thy presence
I am still like the waters
My fears like the morning dew
Evaporate
I am at peace
In thy presence
Of the one my soul loves
My soul, my body at peace
Like the quietness of the morning
I am at peace

    then
 I look up and
 I feel the Lord watching me
Ready to listen to me
Though unworthy I am

I praise him
I worship Him
I adore Him
King of Kings
The one who makes me sing
Songs of Zion

Songs of redemption
The one who holds
Life and death in His hands
The earth and the fullness are yours
The one who lives forever and ever

oh
As I praise Him
I realize my needs are nothing
I realize my problems are nothing
He is able to meet my needs

but
I was created to love Him
I was created to worship Him

Pride

The pride that I am
And I say that I am
Depends on the Lord
Who made me
For I am nothing
I was born nothing
I will die nothing
And my everything
Will be nothing
But my good deeds
Of faith someday
Will be everything

Quiet spirit

When the Holy Spirit
Takes His residence
In my heart

    because
I am purged of sin
I am cleansed of sin
I am sanctified

    then
He creates in me
A listening heart
An obedient heart
An abandoned heart
A directed heart

    that
Seeks not my own
But the will of God
For the glory of God

Rain

Suddenly it darkened
The thunder roared
Like the waves
Heavenly light
Littered the earth
The dark clouds menaced angrily
The drizzle trickled
The torrent shattered angrily
Washing off the dirt
Cleansing off the earth
Then peace settled on earth

     so
After the storms of life
After the trials of life
Comes showers of
     Cleansing
     Blessing

    and
    peace

Relationships

Relationships, Relationships, Relationships
We are born in it
We think in it
We move in it
We work in it

     but
Developing relationships
The complex paradox
Of human nature

     proves
Disastrous
Intriguing
Frustrating
Enigmatic

     only
When we don't try
Develop relationships that remain
When every other thing fades
You will be happy you did
When every other thing fades

Riches

What is my riches
When my life is not rich
When my life like a dry leaf
Squeezed and blown away
And refuses to bloom
And enrich others

What is my riches
When my life is not rich
When my life like a stagnant puddle
Stinks with my riches
And refuses to enrich others

What is my riches
When my life is not rich
When my relationships
Like a scanty leaf
On a summer tree
Yearns for moisture
Of human torch that enriches others

What is my riches
When my life is not rich
When hollow inside
Like a hole in my lungs
Puffs up hot air
That hurts others

Sacrifice

Those who are loved by the Lord
Are those who go the extra mile
To love the Lord with all their heart
And refuse to compromise with sin
Those who love those who hate them
Those who give
When there is nothing to give
Those who forgive
When it seems
 Impossible to forgive
Those who pour their lives to enrich others

             oh
It is the highest calling
Of the Christian faith
Are those who go the extra mile
To glorify him
Regardless of the odds
Regardless of the outcome

Self image

When I was born
My face was hidden
And nobody saw my face
I was left alone
To fain for myself
When I complained
Nobody heard me
My face went inside
And subdued inside
Like a cloth turned backward
My face rumpled inside
Now I am grown
My face refused to change

      oh
If I am born again
Don't turn my face hidden
Turn my face towards you
See my face
Talk to me
Love me
So my face
Will brighten up
My life
My world

Self will

I will says the self
I will through you
Says the Lord

I know says the self
I pour knowledge
Through you
Says the Lord

I have wisdom says the self
I give wisdom
Says the Lord

I own all I have
I loan all you have
Says the Lord

I live without you
Says the self

    oh
You don't understand
I own your life
Says the Lord

Without my Grace
You are nothing
My Grace follows you
All day long
All year long
Says the Lord

Sex

It is easy to love sex
When you desire her
It is easy to love sex
When you can't curb the desire

      but
Remember
She is not like every other thing
That you can cuddle
She like the mermaid dazzles
Like the sirens of Odysseus chants
She is not common
She is not cheap
She is not free

      and
She has a tag
That wears a rag
She has a tag
That poisons inside
She has a tag
That slays outside

oh
It is best to
Leave sex alone
When you are alone
It is best to
Leave sex alone
Unless you are twins
Designed by the Divine

Sin

Sin is more subtle than humans
She is clever than humans
She watches you all the time
She sees you all the time
And comes to you as you are
She knows you
She understands you

        and
Watches out for you
To hurt you
Like a python
To strangle you
When you forget
To watch out for her
Watch out for her
So she does not
Mess you up

        oh
She says she loves you
She actually despises you
Because she is a green eyed woman
Who came down from heaven
And does not want you up in heaven

So
Be careful of her
Be watchful of her
Be alert
Watch like you are dying
Watch like your life hangs on it

        every minute
        every hour
        every day
        every year

For truly
You have nothing on earth
Except heaven
When you leave the earth
You take nothing
Except heaven

Single parenting

Should a child be denied the best
When she could be the best
      Do I care
Confidence, money, sperm bank
I have it all, I can do it all

Should a child be denied the best
When she could be the best
No assets, no money, I walked away
I can't see my child
I can't see my child, I have money

Is it all for the child
The longing for my father
The   hole in my lungs

Solitude

The solitude I dread
For fear inside
So I must face myself
To heal inside
Although I have all fun
I must face myself
To heal inside
For solitude I dread
Conquers the emptiness
I feel inside

The lost Soul

Drown out my emptiness
For fear I drown
My soul to condemn
For I lost myself
For fear I drown
Who sets me free
No one comes near
I know not how
My cage looms
Like a whirl wind
Who sets me free
For I fear I drown

Teaching children

Children are like a wild cat
When they are born
The wild biting
The wild kicking
The unruly nature
The unruly behavior

      then
You begin
The values
The values that shape
The values that mold
Which when rejected
When ignored
Creates the mind
That rises or falls
At the end of time

Teen parenting

She stands like Olympus
She wraps her little bundle
Her eyes glow
Like a twinkle in the dark
They sparkle
Her face a raptured conquest
Her body a quivering trap
Like a cat she purrs
Little woman
Like a dream she glides
Her pompous tower slides
As Pompeii against Caesar
Little imagination
Little fascination
The puddle
The huddle
That looms ahead

Terrorism

I have often wondered
Who is a terrorist
I don't understand
The one who is sad inside
The one who hurts inside
The one who kills outside
The one who has no home inside

      but
I wonder
Are all sad terrorists
Are all who hurt terrorists
I wonder
Who is a terrorist

      look
The one who makes me sad
The one who thinks others less of him
And hurts others
And makes others sad
And refuses to help others
And have the means
To help others
And refuses to understand others

oh
Wipe out terrorists
Who have sad faces
And make me safe
Wipe out terrorists
With guns and make me safe
 Wipe out terrorists
With war and make me safe

I wonder
If that makes me safe
Oh, understand the condition
That makes me sad

then
Wipe out terrorists
Who have sad faces
And terrorists
Will have glad faces
When I understand
Condition that makes me sad

TIME

I often wonder
What is time
Time is elusive
We don't understand it
Time stretches out in infinity
Time is God
God is the end of time
Time is infinite

God a lots time
To finite humans
For His glory
Time has no attachments
Time is free
Nobody questions
What we do with our time
Everyone has the same time

     but
What you do
With your time matters
What you do with your time
Matters someday
What you do with your time
Are recorded now
Though time has no attachments

Time is free
Everybody has the same time

      Oh
Don't waste your time
Is the common thing to say
But a two edge sword
Don't waste your time
Waste it for eternity
Waste it for God
Waste it to lift others
Waste it for the benefit of others
Waste it for the glory of God

      someday
Time will no longer be free
Time will wear a rag
A rag of judgment
A rag of condemnation
When time is weighed
At the end of time
You are found wanting
Or wise
Depending on the quality
Of your time
Depending on the quantity
Of your time

so
Be careful of your time
Use it wisely
Use it for the glory of God
Use it for the benefit of others
Use it for your benefit

Today as a gift from God

Today is a gift from God
Tomorrow may never come
Today finish your work
Tomorrow may never come

Trials

When trials cloud our lives
Then our faith struggles
Our vision obscures
When pain dims the mind
Confusion like a thief
Steals the mind
Then, we can't understand
The way
The way to the light
He bacons us to move on
I know what I am doing
Someday, you will understand

Living the truth

Help me Lord
When I wake up in the morning
When you open my eyes
When you fill my life with new breath
When I know without you
My eyes will not open
Without you, I will be dead
In the morning

    then
Help me to think the truth
Help me to speak the truth
Help me to live the truth
So I may glorify you
Help me Lord

What is truth

What is truth
Truth is life fully enjoyed
It is been true to yourself
It is contentment
It is freedom
Who does not live the truth
Does not have life

but
You ask
What is truth
Truth is God
Living as God designed
Living for Him
Who does not live the truth
Does not have life

for
Life is in the truth
Joy is in the truth
Peace is in the truth
Who lives outside the truth
Lives inside the home of fear

oh
Truth is life
Who does not live the truth
Does not have life
For truth conquers fear
Truth conquers death

Vision

Are you a mirage
Like a silent observer she glides
Possess me she pleads
For want of insight
For want of discernment
Nations stumble and war
Human progress clouds
Opportunities loom
Like a dooms day

     oh
Possess me she pleads
Like an eagle she hopes
She forewarns of dooms day
Possess me she pleads
For want of insight
Life drifters
Like a spider in her web
Shrouded in comfort
So who possess no vision
For vision lodges
In the hearts of few

Waiting on the Lord

The real test of our faith
Is not the prayer
Is not the faith
It is the span of time
When nothing is happening
While we wait

     and
You are tied of waiting
You cry
You pray
You repeat yourself
You storm

     but
Nothing happens
God, are you there
You wonder
He has forsaken me
You wonder

     well
I will do my own thing
There is no God

Many have wondered away
At this point of nothing
They get deceived
They get messed up
They get confused
They come back
Some never come back

    who
Keeps waiting
Is never disappointed
She learns patience
She is blessed

    oh
Waiting on the Lord
Makes the believer
The real test of our faith
Is the span of time
When nothing is happening
While we wait

What we do at this time
Is the real test of our faith
Is who we are in the faith

War

Indulged by modern primitive minds
By nations and societies
Of sophisticated, educated, Kings
Princes, Presidents, States men and Chiefs
But of primitive minds

    who
Are
lustful
 Unenlightened
 Selfish
 Arrogant
 Greedy

    like
Little children
They fight
Plunder
Kill
Rape
Annihilate

    when
They cannot receive
Object of their pleasure
For what does not belong to them

oh
In the end
When primitive game is over
Civilization tumbles over
Primitive minds crumble
For want of wisdom

because
They reject the way of peace
And don't possess the way of peace

What causes war

When I look at the war zone
I wonder why humans go to war
Why do they plunder, kill and vandalize
And wipe off a whole nation
Without a whole thought

It is the foible of human desire
That can't be under human control
It defies conventions and laws
To have its own way
Regardless of consideration
Of human civilization
Regardless of consideration
Of human life

so
Was the mind caged
When desire escaped
I wonder
Who controls desire
So like a wild curb
It does not desire

        but
Desire must think like self control
And wisdom must direct her desire

        then
Desire can love peace
Not war
I wonder
Why humans go to war
For aftermath of war
Doesn't diminish a moment

The will of God

The will of God
Can't be bargained
Can't be changed
Oh, if men knew
That His will
Is His design for men
Before they were created

The will of God
Can't be bargained
Can't be changed
Oh, if men knew
His will is best for them
Is His design for men
Before they were created

The will of God
Can't be bargained
Can't be changed
Oh, if men knew
That His will is
         salvation
         peace
         sanctification
         divine direction
         glorification

      oh
That I may desire His will
That I may desire nothing but His will
Nothing is the same
Nothing is right
If I am not in His will

      remember
His will is what counts
Nothing else counts
Only in His will do things count
My talent
My gifts
My intellect
My money
My beauty
Only in His will do they count

The will of God
Can't be bargained
Can't be changed

Words are daggers

My heart groaned in pain
And refused to rest
The darkness beckoned
My eyelids to rest

     but
The tears dropped
The tears shattered the quietness
The groan echoed in the darkness
The heaviness of my heart pleads

     for
Freedom
Freedom to rest
Oh dear, they hurt
My body riddles with pain
Like a gun shot

     listen
Words are daggers
They kill
They humiliate
They subdue

but
They also heal
If you choose them
Carefully
If you choose them
Wisely

Worship

Stripped naked I stand
Empty open my pretences
The great eye searches
Penitent my heart subdues
For the lump in my heart
Prevents me from singing
I must rid myself of stain
To stand before the Divine
So I waste not my time
The heart sings of Divine love
Not till Divine cleansing
Not till Divine restoration

When I worry

When ever I worry
My heart pounds
My stomach growls
I loose my concentration
I stay a wake all night
I ask myself
Is your anxiety over
No, I still have them
Why did you worry
I won't live long worrying

       so
I analyze my problems
Is it worth dying for
If they are not
If they are
Whether they are or not
 I trust the Lord
I trust the Lord and rest

oh
Trust the Lord
Trusting the Lord
Changes our problems
And the Lord controls the problems
And gives us peace
And gives us answers
In His will
And His will is best
And His will is best for us

Advice to writers

Writers
When you write
Think from your heart
Think original
Think innovative
Think enduring
Thinking makes the difference
Between classic and regular

About writing

Lord, give me the mind to
      write
The strength to
      write
The wisdom to
      write
All for your glory

Your mind

When your mind is messed up
You are truly messed up
You are truly dislocated

and
You will no longer function
You will no longer function as a human being
You are a living dead
You are dead living

so
Be careful
Be careful what you do with your mind
Don't ignore your mind
Your mind is your life
Nourish your mind
Nourish your mind with pure thoughts
Not evil thoughts
Nourish your mind with noble thoughts
Not sinful thoughts

then
You will think pure thoughts
Then you will think noble thoughts
Thoughts of God and His will
Thoughts of goodwill for your neighbor
Thoughts of goodwill for yourself

oh
Your life will change
Because you nourished your mind
With noble thoughts
With pure thoughts

which
Produce   not sinful words
Produce   not sinful actions